**Orchestra
Accompaniment
*series***

The Singer's Gilbert & Sullivan
MEN'S EDITION

On the cover: John Singer Sargent, American, 1856-1925, *Rehearsal of the Pas de Loup Orchestra at the Cirque d'Hiver*, oil on canvas, 1878, 36 $^5/_8$" x 28 $^3/_4$",
Anonymous loan, 81.1972. Copyright © 1996, The Art Institute of Chicago, All Rights Reserved.

ISBN 0-7935-6888-9

**HAL•LEONARD®
CORPORATION**
7777 W. BLUEMOUND RD. P.O. BOX 13819 MILWAUKEE, WI 53213

Orchestra Accompaniment

series

The Singer's Gilbert & Sullivan

MEN'S EDITION

ON THE RECORDING

*John Oakman, tenor
**Richard Halton, baritone
***Steven Page, baritone
Czech Symphony Orchestra conducted by Julian Bigg

with the Prague Philharmonic Choir
Christopher Todd Landor, producer
Eric Tomlinson; Daniel Gable, engineers
recorded at the FHS studios, Prague, 6/92

4

The Gondoliers
or The King of Barataria

Premiered at the Savoy Theatre, London, 7 December 1889. The last successful work by the team of Gilbert & Sullivan, followed by only two more collaborations: Utopia Limited (1893) and *The Grand Duke* (1896).

The Duke of Plaza-Toro arrives in Venice in desperate financial circumstances. He reveals to his daughter Casilda that she was wed to the son of the King of Barataria when the two were still infants. Furthermore, the boy in question must now assume the throne, since an uprising has killed his father. This is all good news to the Duke, but not to Casilda, for she and her father's drummer Luiz are in love. More bad news follows: The king in question is one of two gondoliers, Marco and Giuseppe, who were raised as brothers—but the woman who was their nursemaid must be obtained to determine which is which. As if this weren't enough, both young men are newly married to a couple of nice Venetian girls. While all wait for the return of the nursemaid, Marco and Giuseppe go to Barataria to rule jointly. There they quickly miss their wives. Marco sings of the delights of female companionship ("Take a Pair of Sparkling Eyes"). By and by, everyone converges on Barataria—the young brides, the Duke and his retinue, and the nursemaid, who reveals that she had done some baby-swapping of her own, and that the real king is neither Marco nor Giuseppe, but the boy she raised as her son: Luiz! General rejoicing ensues, mixed with some regret as the two gondoliers leave their kingdom and return to the canals of Venice.

H.M.S. Pinafore
or The Lass That Loved a Sailor

Premiered at the Opera Comique, London, 25 May 1878. The first of Gilbert & Sullivan's "big three" comic operas (along with *The Pirates of Penzance* and *The Mikado*) and the one that established their reputation.

The beauty of satire is that it can mock both sides of an issue. Here the twin targets are the inviolable British class structure and the accompanying naïve pretensions of egalitarianism. The curtain rises on Her Majesty's ship Pinafore, newly docked in Portsmouth and preparing for inspection by Sir Joseph Porter, First Lord of the Admiralty. When Sir Joseph arrives on board, he tells of his rise from office boy to "the ruler of the Queen's Navee" ("When I Was a Lad I Served a Term"). Captain Corcoran, commander of the Pinafore, has arranged for his daughter Josephine to wed Sir Joseph, though she is secretly in love with Ralph Rackstraw, a common sailor. Sir Joseph talks a good game about equality, but in the end—after numerous turns of plot and the obligatory cases of mistaken identity—he, along with everyone else, is constrained, even comforted, by the boundaries of class.

Iolanthe

or The Peer and the Peri

Premiered at the Savoy Theatre, London, 25 November 1882. The first of the "Savoy operas"—those that opened at Richard D'Oyly Carte's Savoy Theatre.

Iolanthe, a fairy, had committed the capital offense of marrying a mortal, but was granted exile rather than death. After twenty-five years, the fairy Queen allows her to rejoin elfin society. Meanwhile, Iolanthe's son Strephon, who is half fairy (from the waist up) has fallen in love with young Phyllis, ward of the Lord Chancellor. But the latter will not consent to their marriage. In fact, he's been trying, unsuccessfully, to petition himself for her hand, and the turmoil is giving him nightmares ("When You're Lying Awake with a Dismal Headache"). In the end, Iolanthe clears the way for Strephon and Phyllis to be wed by appealing to the Lord Chancellor, who turns out to be her husband, and who had believed her to be dead. When the entire the fairy court reveals that they have married the House of Lords, the fairy Queen is in a quandary: she can't sentence them all to death. Fortunately, the Lord Chancellor, experienced in these matters, changes fairy law with a quick bit of legislative chicanery, the Lords all sprout wings, and everyone flies off happily to Fairyland.

The Mikado

or The Town of Titipu

Premiered at the Savoy Theatre, London, 14 March 1885. The best-known of the Gilbert & Sullivan collaborations, it has been called the most popular opera of all time.

Into the town of Titipu rushes Nanki-Poo, who introduces himself to the populace ("A Wand'ring Minstrel I") before stating his business: he seeks news of Yum-Yum, his true love. Alas, she is to be married that very afternoon to Ko-Ko, the Lord High Executioner. Ko-Ko enters to general acclaim. He has no intention of executing anyone, ever, for in truth he is next in line for the chopping block. Nevertheless, if a victim were needed, he's "got a little list" of annoying candidates ("As Some Day It May Happen"). Unfortunately for him, that day has arrived, for word comes from the Mikado, the emperor of Japan, that someone must be executed, and soon. Ko-Ko finds a willing subject in Nanki-Poo, who, contemplating suicide rather than life without Yum-Yum, agrees to be beheaded instead, under the condition that he first be allowed a month as Yum-Yum's husband. The young lovers wed, and Ko-Ko ultimately agrees to pretend the execution has taken place without actually performing it. All seems well until the Mikado himself appears, accompanied by the spinster Katisha. She's long had her sights set on Nanki-Poo, who it turns out is no troubadour, but the Mikado's son. The only way to avert her wrath is for Ko-Ko to woo her, which, reluctantly, he does ("Willow, Tit-Willow"), and marry her himself. In this lampoon of corruption in government, even underhanded officials can eventually bring about a happy ending.

The Pirates of Penzance

or The Slave of Duty

Premiered at the Fifth Avenue Theatre, New York, 31 December 1879. The only one of Gilbert & Sullivan's works to have its official premiere outside London, it did in fact receive one prior performance in England for purposes of copyright registration.

Twenty-one-year-old Frederic, bound by his sense of duty to serve out his apprenticeship to a band of pirates, has reached the end of his indentures and decides henceforth to oppose the cutthroat crew rather than join them. After leaving the pirates, Frederic happens upon a party of young women and appeals to them for pity ("Oh, Is There Not One Maiden Breast"). The pirates then arrive on the scene, determined to marry the young ladies, but the girls' father, Major-General Stanley, enters just in time ("I Am the Very Model of a Modern Major-General") and wins clemency by claiming to be an orphan. Frederic, at first duty-bound to destroy his former comrades, rejoins them when he finds that his apprenticeship extends to his twenty-first birthday, and, having been born on February 29, he has so far had only five birthdays. But in the end, the pirates yield to the police at the invocation of Queen Victoria's name, and when it is revealed that they are actually wayward noblemen, they earn their pardon and permission to marry the Major-General's daughters.

Take a Pair of Sparkling Eyes
from THE GONDOLIERS

Words by W.S. Gilbert

Music by Arthur Sullivan

Take my coun - sel, hap - py man!

Act up - on it, if you can, if you can, if you

cresc.

f *con forza*

can, Act up - on it, if you can, ___ hap - py man,

if ___ you can! ___

When I Was a Lad I Served a Term
from H.M.S. PINAFORE

Words by W.S. Gilbert

Music by Arthur Sullivan

po-lished up the han-dle of the big front door.
co-pied all the let-ters in a big round hand.

I
I

CHORUS:

He po-lished up the han-dle of the big front door.
He co-pied all the let-ters in a big round hand.

He po-lished up the han-dle of the big front door.
He co-pied all the let-ters in a big round hand.

po-lished up that han-dle so care-ful-lee, That now I am the ru-ler of the Queen's Na-vee!
co-pied all the let-ters in a hand so free, That now I am the ru-ler of the Queen's Na-vee!

He
He

He
He

po-lish'd up that han-dle so care-ful-lee That now he is the ru-ler of the Queen's Na-vee!
co-pied all the let-ters in a hand so free, That now he is the ru-ler of the Queen's Na-vee!

po-lish'd up that han-dle so care-ful-lee That now he is the ru-ler of the Queen's Na-vee!
co-pied all the let-ters in a hand so free, That now he is the ru-ler of the Queen's Na-vee!

SIR J. PORTER:

3. In ser-ving writs I made such a name That an
4. Of le-gal know-ledge I ac-quired such a grip That they

ar-ti-cled clerk I soon be-came; I wore clean col-lars and a bran' new suit For the
took me in-to the part-ner-ship, And that jun-ior part-ner-ship I ween Was the

14

SIR J. PORTER:

5. I grew so rich that I was sent By a
6. Now lands-men all, who - ev - er you may be, If you

pock - et bor - ough in - to Par - lia - ment. I al - wys vo - ted at my par - ty's call, And I
want to rise — to the top of the tree, If your soul is - n't fet - tered to an of - fice stool, Be

nev - er thought of think-ing for my - self at all.
care - ful to be guid - ed by this gold - en rule,

I
Stick

CHORUS:

He nev - er thought of think-ing for him - self at all.
Be care - ful to be guid - ed by this gold - en rule.

He nev - er thought of think-ing for him - self at all.
Be care - ful to be guid - ed by this gold - en rule.

When You're Lying Awake with a Dismal Headache
from IOLANTHE

Words by W.S. Gilbert

Music by Arthur Sullivan

last, and the night has been long— dit - to, dit - to my

cresc.

a piacere

song— And thank good - ness they're both of them o -

f *colla voce*

(Lord Chancellor falls exhausted on a seat.)

ver!

Con fuoco

ff

A Wand'ring Minstrel I
from THE MIKADO

Words by W.S. Gilbert

Music by Arthur Sullivan

*In a solo performance with piano this can be an instrumental interlude.

sail - or ___ sees Is when he's down At an in - land ___ town, With his Nan - cy on his

knees, yeo - ho! And his arm ___ a - round her waist! Then man the cap - stan–

CHORUS:

off we go, As the fid - dler swings us round, With a

yeo heave - ho, And a rum ___ be - low, Hur - rah for the home - ward

As Some Day It May Happen
from THE MIKADO

Words by W.S. Gilbert

Music by Arthur Sullivan

write for au - to - graphs —   All   peo - ple who have flab - by hands and
thu - si - as - tic   tone,   All   cen - tu - ries but   this, and ev - 'ry

ir - ra - tat - ing   laughs —   All   chil - dren who are   up in   dates, and
coun - try but   his   own;   And   the   la - dy from the prov - in - ces, who

floor you   with 'em   flat —   All   per - sons who in shak - ing hands, shake
dress - es like   a   guy,   And "who does - n't think she danc - es, but would

hands with you   like *that* —   And   all   third per - sons who   on spoil - ing
rath - er like   to   try";   And that   sin - gu - lar a - nom - a - ly,   the

CHORUS
OF MEN:

tête-à-têtes in-sist — They'd none of 'em be missed — they'd none of 'em be missed! *He's
la-dy nov-el-ist — I don't think she'd be missed — I'm *sure* she'd not be missed! He's

got 'em on the list — he's got 'em on the list; And they'll
got her on the list — he's got her on the list; And I

KO-KO:

none of 'em be missed — they'll none of 'em be missed!
don't think she'll be missed — I'm *sure* she'll not be missed!

2. There's the
3. And that

Ni-si Pri-us nui-sance, who just now is rath-er rife, The ju-di-cial hu-mor-ist — I've

*Performed as a solo with piano, this section is an instrumental interlude.

rath - er leave to *you.* But it real - ly does - n't mat - ter whom you

CHORUS OF MEN:

put up - on the list, For they'd none of 'em be missed — they'd none of 'em be missed! You may

put 'em on the list — you may put 'em on the list; And they'll none of 'em be missed — they'll

none of 'em be missed!

Willow, Tit-Willow
from THE MIKADO

Words by W.S. Gilbert

Music by Arthur Sullivan

bird - ie?" I cried, "Or a rath - er tough worm in your lit - tle in - side?" With a

shake of his poor lit - tle head he re - plied, "Oh, wil - low, tit - wil - low, tit -

wil - low!" _ 2. He slapped at his chest, as he

sat on that bough, Sing - ing "Wil - low, tit - wil - low, tit - wil - low!" _ And a

cold per - spi - ra - tion be - span - gled his brow, Oh, wil - low, tit - wil - low, tit - wil - low! __ He __

sobbed and he sighed, and a gur - gle he gave, Then he plunged him - self in - to the

bil - low - y wave, And an ech - o a - rose from the su - i - cide's grave– "Oh, wil - low, tit - wil - low, tit -

wil - low!" __

3. Now I feel just as sure as I'm

sure that my name Is-n't Wil-low, tit - wil-low, tit - wil-low, That 'twas blight-ed af - fec - tion that

made him ex-claim, "Oh, wil-low, tit - wil-low, tit - wil-low!" _ And if you re-main cal - lous and

ob - du - rate, I Shall _ per - ish as he did, and you will know why, Though I

prob - a - bly shall not ex - claim as I die, "Oh, wil-low, tit - wil-low, tit - wil-low!" _

pp

Ped. *

I Am the Very Model of a Modern Major-General
from THE PIRATES OF PENZANCE

Words by W.S. Gilbert

Music by Arthur Sullivan

order cat - e - gor - i - cal; I'm ver - y well ac - quaint - ed, too, with mat - ters math - e - mat - i - cal, I
ar - i - ties pa - rab - i - lous; I can tell un - doubt - ed Ra - pha - els from Ger - ard Dows and Zof - fa - nies I

un - der - stand e - qua - tions, both the sim - ple and quad - rat - i - cal, A - bout bi - no - mial the - o - rem I'm
know the croak - ing cho - rus from the *Frogs* of Ar - is - toph - a - nes! Then I can hum a fugue of which I've

(Bothered for next rhyme– struck with an idea– joyfully)

teem - ing with a lot o' news, With man - y cheer - ful facts a - bout the
heard the mu - sic's din a - fore, And whis - tle all the airs from that in -

CHORUS:

ƒ

square of the hy - pot - e - nuse. With man - y cheer - ful facts a - bout the square of the hy - pot - e - nuse, With
fer - nal non - sense, *Pin - a - fore!* And whis - tle all the airs from that in - fer - nal non - sense, *Pin - a - fore,* And

ƒ

With man - y cheer - ful facts a - bout the square of the hy - pot - e - nuse, With
And whis - tle all the airs from that in - fer - nal non - sense, *Pin - a - fore,* And

* *ƒ*

*Cut to ** when performing as a solo with piano.

CHORUS:

am the ver - y mod - el of a mod - ern Ma - jor - Gen - er - al. In short, in mat - ters veg - e - ta - ble,

an - i - mal, and min - er - al, He is the ver - y mod - el of a mod - ern Ma - jor - Gen - er - al.

Slower

MAJOR:

3. In fact, when I know what is meant by

"mam - e - lon" and "rav - e - lin", When I can tell at sight a Mau - ser ri - fle from a jav - e - lin, When

such af-fairs as sor-ties and sur-pris-es I'm more wa-ry at, And when I know pre-cise-ly what is

meant by "com-mis-sa-ri-at", When I have learnt what prog-ress has been made in mod-ern gun-ner-y, When

I know more of tac-tics than a nov-ice in a nun-ner-y– In short, when I've a smat-ter-ing of

(Bothered for a rhyme– struck with an idea)

Vivace

el-e-men-tal strat-e-gy– You'll say a bet-ter Ma-jor-Gen-er-

*Cut to ** when performing as a solo with piano.

*Cut to ** when performing as a solo with piano.

Oh, Is There Not One Maiden Breast
from THE PIRATES OF PENZANCE

Words by W.S. Gilbert

Music by Arthur Sullivan

54

*When performed as a solo with piano, a cut may be made to **.

is there not one maid - en here Whose home - ly face and bad com -

plex - ion Have caused all hope to dis - ap - pear Of

ev - er win - ning man's af - fec - tion? To such an one, If

such there be, I swear, by heav - en's arch a - bove you, If